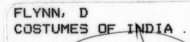

COSTUMES
OF
INDIA

DORRIS FLYNN

TRICOLOUR BOOKS
LONDON

© 1985 Dorris Flynn

Illustrated by Horilal
Layout by Annada Munshi
The author wishes to thank Nalini Barua,
Prafullo Dutta and Sujit Banerjee.

Published by Shreeram Vidyarthi for
Tricolour Books (A Division of Books from India UK Ltd)
at 45 Museum Street, London WC1A 1LR
in arrangement with Oxford & IBH Publishing Co.,
66 Janpath, New Delhi 110001, India

ISBN 1 85127 048 5

Printed in India

THE author wishes to thank all her friends whose devoted encouragement has been inspiring and deeply appreciated. She extends special thanks to her husband, for without his support, this book could not have been written.

Costumes of India

CONTENTS

FOREWORD

IN December of 1968, I came to live in India. I had been in India before for two visits, one in 1962, the other in 1965. On both occasions I was very impressed by the beautiful saris worn by Indian women, and by the fact that I did not see any two saris alike. At that time I did not know the area from which a lady came could be identified by the sari she wore.

After making friends in India, I became aware of the many types of dress, and the manner in which they are worn. To those foreign to India, all saris seem the same—this is not so. There are numerous ways of draping and wrapping this costume, each originating in a different part of the country. Also there are many fabrics, weaves and designs which denote the area of origin.

The purpose of this book is to show a few of the costumes worn.

The Author

PREFACE

THE costumes of India, colourful and thrilling in their endless variety, are a fascinating subject. Any study of it must necessarily involve a continuous story of an evolved appeal and technique, from the time when man started wearing clothes to the present day. This evolution is as natural and spontaneous as the thinking of the human mind or as human breathing. Indian costumes have taken their own shape and form, as elsewhere, according to the climatic, social and even political changes that mark the vast span of the Indian territory, and also the vicissitudes of its long history. They have changed and are still changing according to taste and utility, yet they are tied to their old moorings of ancient traditions on the one hand, and influenced on the other, by the unavoidable contacts with the outer world at the present day. Against this perspective only, Indian costumes are to be studied and described.

One of the first publications on the subject came in 1950 by G. S. Ghuriye entitled INDIAN COSTUME, which dealt with the subject historically from the earliest times. This was followed by a work by Jamila Brij Bhusan in 1958, under the title: THE COSTUMES AND TEXTILES OF INDIA, followed by yet another, a more concentrated one: COSTUMES OF INDIA AND PAKISTAN by S. N. Dar, published in 1969. These works deal with the subject with a mass of historical material behind, drawn from literature, religious, mythological and secular. The illustrations are mainly as pieces of costumes and are detached from the human element. The treatment is not much different also in Charles Fabri's A HISTORY OF INDIAN DRESS, which appeared in the meanwhile, in 1960. As distinct from this kind of approach with overwhelming material and the emotional standpoint of the Indian authors, Dorris Flynn from America, who has lived in India, and admired the country's rich variety of costumes with a thrill typical of a foreigner, has dealt with the subject with a most personal touch. Her admiration, and envy, if I may say so, for the colourful dresses of the ladies of this land, are mingled with a critical approach and a sense of grace and dignity. Here in this presentation, the examples shown as wearing the types of costumes are drawn from actual life and portrayed in a deft hand by Shri Horilal, already well-known for his sketches of Indian life and ancient traditions of this country, and have, therefore, a special claim on the attention and appreciation of those interested in the subject. The illustrations depicting the inseparable personalities taken from the life of the people in their natural settings and in their normal daily engagements, bring about an intimate touch in them. Done mostly in life-drawing, these provide a lyrical element in the rustic background of the village hut, the green meadows, the flowing rivulet and the cultivated land beyond, for these dressed women. Indeed, costumes go with the personality, and in India it is more so. And Dorris Flynn, with the help of the artist, has caught this personality for us, as though in a camera. The text is subordinated, the dynamism of the personalities depicted brought out to the full, with the costumes aiding the whole development in their vividness and in their colour.

27 Jawaharlal Nehru Road
Calcutta-13

(A. K. BHATTACHARYYA)
Director, Indian Museum

ABOUT THE AUTHOR

THE author has written this book to show some of the costumes of one of the worlds most interesting countries—India. Dorris Flynn was born in Baltimore, Maryland, U.S.A. She received a Bachelor of Science degree in education from the Maryland State College and taught school until her marriage. She was active in light opera and theatre groups.

The writer and her husband, who is with the overseas division of a large American Automotive Company, have lived in many countries and have travelled throughout the world. It was while living in India that she became interested in the varieties of clothing she saw in her travels within this vast country. She visited libraries and art museums in search of information on Indian costumes. At the Academy of Fine Arts in Calcutta she met Horilal, one of India's most promising young artists, and the idea for a book on Indian fashions was born.

This book, with its pen and ink sketches and water color paintings by the artist, and the literary efforts of the Author, shows some of the fascinating Costumes of India.

INTRODUCTION

THE picture of the Indian woman familiar to a foreigner is a figure draped with a long flowing piece of cloth, half of it wrapped around the waist falling floor length as an improvised skirt, the remaining half climbing up over the bust which is clothed in a close fitting blouse.

The long piece of cloth is the famous sari of India. Its charm lies in the fact that it plays down the wearer's sex, and yet is the most feminine of all female costumes in the world.

Diversity, however, is the very soul of this vast country of over five hundred million. When a newcomer arrives in India, he realizes for the first time that the sari is only one of the many garments worn in different parts of the country. The great variety of dresses, like the numerous languages, gives the impression of not one, but many countries. Even the sari is worn in a countless number of ways.

The costumes of Indian women can broadly be classified under four headings:

1. The sari—a length of material, looking more or less like a very long scarf, worn with a loose bodice, called a blouse.

2. The ghagra—a profusely pleated skirt reaching the ankles, worn with a tight bodice known as the choli, and a veil like scarf.

3. The salwar—tight fitting trousers made of soft material, worn with the kameez, which is a long tunic reaching mid-thigh, flared at the end and having long tapering sleeves. This ensemble, too, has a scarf of fine material thrown over the bosom.

4. The sarong—a shorter length of cotton (or silk) worn around the breast below the armpits, reaching halfway between knee and ankle.

Historically, the most interesting fact about the garments of India, male or female, is that for a long time tailoring was unknown in the country. The use of scissors and the needle to cut and sew up pieces of cloth to make dresses came probably with the Muslims. The main surviving pieces of the traditional garments are the sari for the female and the dhoti for the male which are untailored.

The costumes of India, as they stand today, are the products of two main influences, Muslim and Western. The Western influence is more marked in male clothing, but for the women it is limited to the evolution of the blouse and the acceptance of the brassier and the winter coat. Also the entire wardrobe of children's attire, today, is an import from the West.

What the Indian woman calls her blouse is a variation of the older close-fitting bodice called choli. Although it follows the lines of the Western blouse, it is not exactly the same. Except for these, the Indian woman stands apart in the whole East in rejecting Western dress. In urban India the Western slacks and shirt, sometimes with jacket and necktie, have virtually ousted the traditional male costumes, not so with the female. Barring a handful of Indians of Eurasian origin, women, including those who otherwise accept the West in total, never dream of trying the Western skirt. Sari or salwar, ghagra or sarong, it is always and everywhere the traditional Indian costume.

Rarely do we see a woman of any other country outside her native land in her national dress. Yet, it is almost impossible to find an Indian woman abroad in any costume except the sari and choli. That is the Indian woman.

Dorrie Flynn

TRADITIONAL INDIAN DRESS

SARI
BLOUSE
CHOLI
GHAGRA
SALWAR-KAMEEZ
ORHNA

THE SARI : HOW TO WEAR IT.

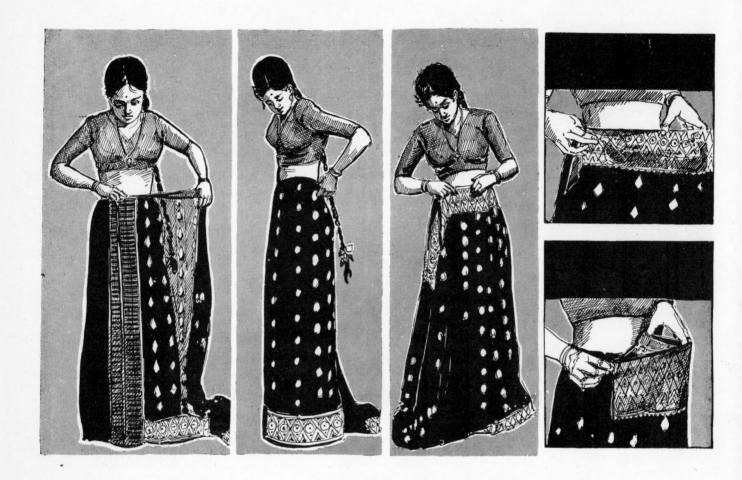

THE sari is a length of cotton or silk, a yard and a third wide, with two borders, one along each side of the length. There is an art of draping the female figure with the material.

The art, so subtle and delicate, is manifest in the pleats and folds, and in the magic that conceals the shortcomings of the figure, but emphasizes the strong points. It is easy for the woman who knows the art—and in fact every Indian woman is proficient in it.

The most expensive silk saris of Banaras may be elaborately woven all over in real gold, and cost a fortune. The intricate designs in the texture, along the borders, and the showy crosswise border (known as pallu in some parts and anchla in others), show Indian craftsmanship at its highest. Even the cheapest cotton sari, with two plain red or orange borders, draped with care, may adorn the wearer with a beauty of its own which neither gold nor silk can give.

The sari is worn in a great variety of ways. The length naturally varies according to the style, the maximum being ten yards. The standard length for the style now accepted all over India as national, is six yards. The superiority of this style is beyond question, and has induced women in non-sari areas to wear this garment.

In this style, the sari is worn over a petticoat, which is an under-skirt, slightly gathered as 'A' line and held by a string tied tightly at the waist. After the choli and petticoat are fitted in place, half of the sari, without the decorative crosswise border, is placed around the waist.

A length sufficient for one wrap around the waist is first taken, and tucked into the petticoat. From the point where it is tucked in, another length is taken to be gathered into pleats. The pleated portion is also tucked in, and the remaining half is then passed up over the bust, gathered in neat lengthwise folds, and let fall over the left shoulder to reach the hip. The decorative crosswise border is displayed either wholly on the back or is fanned out to show half in front and half on the hip.

BLOUSE CHOLI

THE upper garment that goes with the sari is a blouse, although somewhat different from a blouse in the Western sense. It is a bodice developed from an earlier indigenous garment which used to be worn next to the skin as a breast support. The earlier garment was called choli, and even now, after its evolution to the present form, it is called choli as well as blouse.

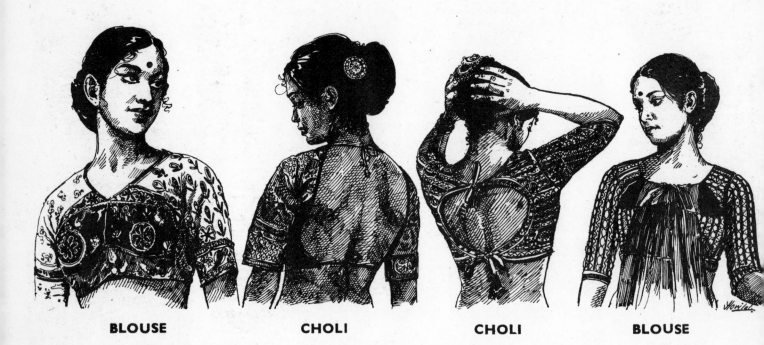

BLOUSE **CHOLI** **CHOLI** **BLOUSE**

The earlier choli was worn in parts of North, West and South India, but was not universally used. For those who wore it, it was the only upper garment, serving as a breast support. Now the brassier is used.

The original choli has not disappeared. In some remote places it still survives in traditional costumes. There are several types, one being low backed with back-fasteners, and the other front-fastened, with a covered back.

The blouse, unlike the sari, lends to some tailoring skill and has room for individuality by way of novelties in neck-lines, sleeves and embroidery. The modern tendency is towards a shorter length showing much of the midriff. The bare midriff was a style indigenous to certain areas, but at present it is popular in the whole country, and is one of the noticeable features in the national ensemble.

GHAGRA ORHNA

GHAGRA AND SHORT SARI

KAMEEZ–GHAGRA WITH ORHNA

SALWAR–KAMEEZ AND ORHNA

GHAGRA

IN large areas of western and northern India, and also partly in the south, the main lower garment is the ghagra, a kind of "maxi" skirt reaching to the ankles, and marked by lots of vertical pleats. It is worn below the navel, and is held up by a draw string.

The ghagra may take as many as twenty, or even thirty yards of cloth. In one variety it is narrow at the waist and flared at the bottom end. This type is made by sewing together triangular pieces. The other type is fashioned out of rectangular pieces, or by pleating and gathering one single piece of twenty yards or so. This is more puffed at the waist and is more or less bell-shaped.

The ghagra is worn with a choli for the upper garment. Sometimes a briefer edition of the choli called kachuli is worn with a ghagra. The choli may be either back or front fastened. The combination needs a third piece, which is a scarf, to complement the choli and ghagra. It is known by various local names such as orhna, dupatta or chunari.

SALWAR-KAMEEZ

THE salwar is a pair of trousers, either loose or close fitting, something like the nineteenth century drawers of the Western women, minus their frills. They are extra long to make the trouser ends wrinkle just above the ankles. The salwar, which is of soft material is generally white, but can also be a color or print in mod fashions.

The kameez is a long tunic reaching mid-thigh with tapering sleeves or sleeveless. It is generally flared at the bottom, or hobbled in the very modern version. This ensemble is figure fitting and somewhat revealing. Next to the sari and blouse of the national ensemble, it is the most widely liked combination. But for its exacting demands on the figures it might have been the teenager's exclusive in the whole country. Otherwise, it almost enjoys the status of an alternative national ensemble. The salwar-kameez is never complete without the scarf thrown over the bosom. Modern variations of this ensemble are now the rage in many western countries.

ORHNA

THE orhna is a scarf, usually measuring seven feet six inches long and four feet six inches wide. It is made of fine silk or cotton and used as a veil to cover the head and face, as respect, when in the presence of parents-in-law. Sometimes it is worn with a short sari to make up for the short flowing free end. Another way to use the orhna is with the ghagra. Here one end is tucked into the center of the waist and the other end is passed over to the back from the left and then drawn up to rest on the head. One corner of this end is passed under the right armpit from the back and tucked into the front of the choli or ghagra at the left waist.

Still another use of the orhna is for it to rest on the bosom with two ends flung over the shoulders. This version is worn with the salwar and kameez of Punjab.

Orhnas may be plain or decorative. One very popular variety is the tie-and-dye type. Many are spangled with shining tinsels.

West Bengal

AFTER living in India for only a short time I became conscious of the delightful variety of women's dress styles. Being extremely interested in regional difference in women's fashions, I was attracted and even bewildered by the diversities of color, pattern and style in feminine attire. My thoroughly occidental background—although relieved by a fair amount of travel in other parts of the world—provided no clue for identifying the geographical origin of Indian women, of either high or modest station, by their clothing. I soon became aware of the fact that Indian women are understandably proud of those origins and are careful to identify these through their dress styles.

Even in Calcutta which was my new home, I had no way of distinguishing a woman of this state, of which the city is the capital, from one from Bombay or Delhi, by just looking at her sari. As in many parts of India, the sari is not the only dress for all women of West Bengal. Some groups have their own traditional costumes in which the sari has no place at all.

Geographically, this state forms the central part of the eastern zone of the country. It is the Indian section of a large single province now divided, the eastern portion having become part of Pakistan.

The hill districts in the north—one including the city of Darjeeling, a name familiar to foreign tourists—have borders with Nepal, Bhutan and Sikkim. They are inhabited by tribes with strong Mongoloid features, each speaking its own tongue. In their dress, women of these tribes show a closer affinity with Nepal, Bhutan and even Tibet than with the rest of West Bengal.

The tribes inhabiting the western border districts in West Bengal are naturally influenced in their dress by the neighboring people of Bihar and Orissa.

The plains just below the hilly north have been the homes, from the very early times of Indian history, of groups now speaking dialects of Bengali. Racially, they have features recalling many South-east Asian peoples. The main feature of the costume of their women is that they are surprisingly like the sarong of Java. It consists of a broad piece of cloth about four yards long wrapped around the upper portion of the body just below the armpits and tucked in tightly. The lower end reaches half way between the knees and the ankles. There is no separate piece, therefore, to cover the breasts. Arms and shoulders are left bare and there is no covering for the head, even for married women.

In the eyes of these plains people, the Bengalis down south are aliens. But long contact and a standard education had their effects, and today their women readily take to the conventional sari-and-blouse ensemble.

Unless she is aggressively mod, the average educated Bengali girl, dressed according to her own style of wearing the sari, breathes a refined taste. The quality of the material also shows her refinement. Her sari may be made of the plainest yarn, and lack color and decorations, but she will stand out in a crowd with an unadorned elegance that does not fail to attract really appreciative eyes. It may be an inner light which her generally unimpressive vital statistics cannot dim, or it may be a sweetness and softness the moisture characteristic of the local climate gives her. As the story goes, a Mughal emperor's son, when banished to Bengal, could not be lured back to the bejewelled grandeur of Delhi, because, according to the prince, "Delhi's wealth is paled down to insignificance compared to a crown of flowers made by a Bengali gardener's daughter."

In what may be called her negligee, the Bengali girl shows a preference for subdued shades, with neat and artistic motifs. She prefers the cool tones of sky blue or foliage green, and orange is among the warm colors she likes. The free end of her sari is drawn from the right hip to cover the bosom diagonally, and goes over the left shoulder, to return to the front from under the right armpit. The remaining portion, up to the end, is then again thrown over the left shoulder. Married women draw the sari up from under the left armpit to cover the head from behind, like a hood, after the first diagonal wrap. The remaining length is allowed to fall from over the right shoulder.

In formal wear, the Bengali woman displays the decorative crosswise border, half in front, and half on the hip. In north India the border shows wholly on the front, elsewhere on the hip.

It is interesting to note that only about a century ago, a Bengali Hindu woman wore no separate upper garment. The free end of the sari was draped around the torso twice to give the breasts a double cover. The northern, central and western parts of India were the first to adopt an upper piece, probably from contact with West Asians. The other parts, including West Bengal, were slow to follow.

In West Bengal, the predecessor of today's blouse was imported by the British after the conquest, but not until the latter half of the nineteenth century was the blouse to be accepted by the Bengali woman. The first to use it were those Hindus who broke away from the traditional religion, because it stood in their way to higher education in Western countries. A Hindu returning from an overseas journey was an outcast. This induced many Hindus to become Christians. Later, progressive Hindus formed themselves into a sect by reforming their own religion in a Christian mold, calling it Brahma. Brahma women could accept Western education, which Hindu women resisted. They readily took to the European blouse, which was criticized by orthodox Hindus as obscene. To a Hindu woman of Bengal, even the suggestion of wearing a blouse (or shoes for that matter) was a sacrilege. These, according to them, were things which only public women needed. It did not, however, take the English blouse long to find its place in the wardrobe of the Hindu woman. So today it is, without question, the upper garment of Bengali women. Habit dies hard; even today it is not difficult to find in rural areas, or in small towns, Bengali women who think nothing of going outdoors with only the sari to serve both as lower and upper garment.

The dream of a young Bengali girl of a family of average means is to have a beautiful Banaras sari in her wardrobe. Whether or not there is an ancient tradition behind it, today it is almost a must to include a Banaras sari among the bride's gifts. So the Banaras sari to her is symbolic of all the romance of marriage.

The European influence made another important addition to the wardrobe of the Indian woman. It was the chemise, a gown-like garment with short sleeves, which served as a combined breast covering and petticoat. For formal occasions, it was used in Bengal as an under garment with a blouse worn over it. For casual wear, only the chemise was worn. It reigned supreme in Bengal until the appearance of the European bra in about the forties. Now only older women use the chemise. The bra has almost swept the chemise out of use in India.

BATHING BEAUTY

Village girl emerging from a pond bath, carrying home a pitcher of water, in a dripping wet sari clinging to her body. She has ever been a favorite subject with poets and painters.

A RURAL SETTING

The village is in West Bengal, but the sari style of the girl (inset) is more of the neighboring state, Bihar. A common feature in border areas.

PERIOD COSTUME Late nineteenth century picture shows a bride of a well-to-do husband posing for a photograph. The sari drawn over the head serves as a framing to the face, as well as a veil used to cover the face when meeting in-laws.

VILLAGE GIRL The absence of a separate upper garment is still common in West Bengal. A plain sari is wrapped around to cover the body. For physical work it is worn a few inches above the ankle, the free end being wound around the waist tightly.

OLD FASHIONED GIRL

In dress of fifty years ago.

THE WELL-TO-DO

The very rich have elaborately furnished dressing rooms with large expensive mirrors and beauty aids, all imported. Dressing up ends with feet being bordered with a red dye, a traditional practice which has survived even in modern times.

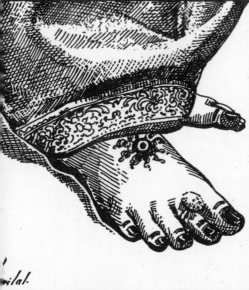

ADORNED FEET

Especially decorated for a gay occasion.

24

THE NEW BRIDE The bridal dress consists of a costly
Banaras sari, a brocade blouse, a veil, and a head-dress
made of the pith of a native water plant.

1

2

3

4

Costumes of yesterday

OLD FASHION
New bride at home of in-laws. Right: Now a member of the in-law's household, she lifts her veil to uncover her eyes.

.2 FOR A GAY EVENING
A modern Bengali girl dressed for fancy dress ball.

3-4 BRITISH INFLUENCE
Brahma women in saris and lace blouses imported by Europeans in the mid-nineteenth century. These were the first blouses; later they were accepted by Hindu women all over Bengal.

HARVEST DANCE

A Tripura girl dressed for a folk-dance invoking blessings for a good harvest.

Assam

ASSAM is a name the average tourist is apt to know even before he has formed a clear picture of India. It is in this state the famous game preserve at Kaziranga is found, where people from the world over come to meet the celebrated one-horned Indian rhinoceros.

This state, along with Manipur, Nagaland, Meghalaya and the North East Frontier Agency (NEFA), with which it has close cultural and other affinities, forms the easternmost sector of India, having borders with Burma and East Pakistan. Its physical geography is one of the most fascinating in the country, with its extremely rich landscape, endless tracts of dense green forests, its blue mountains, lush grassy plains, and its deep, wide, rapid rivers. Nature is wild and virgin here. Its beauty has a pristine freshness not matched elsewhere. The luxuriant monsoon forests are among the world's richest sources of interesting flora and fauna. Its vegetation is composed of trees and plants which represent all climatic zones from tropical to temperate. The orchids and lilies are of the most enchanting hues. Its wild life includes elephant, tiger, wild buffalo and rhinoceros.

In such a magnificent setting dwell people whose dress makes a most interesting study for students of design. It is interesting because there are so many tribal groups and sub-groups inhabiting the State, that a number of distinctive costumes appear. Because of the great diversity of the dresses of the numerous tribes of Assam, it is possible only to note the colorful features of some principal tribes.

There is one ensemble that can be called the traditional costume of the Assamese women. It is known as the mekhala and chadar. The dresses of most Assamese women, whichever tribe they may belong to, can be called variations of the mekhala and chadar. In areas having borders with Bengal, the sari exists side by side with the mekhala and chadar, but the latter is the only dress that can be said to represent Assam.

The mekhala and chadar consists of two pieces. The first is a straight cut skirt worn around the waist reaching to the ankles. It is made of a rectangular piece of cloth, three yards by one yard. The lower half of the skirt is richly embroidered and can be of cotton or silk—a variety of Assam silk called muga. The chadar is another length of cloth, also embroidered, which is wrapped around the upper half of the body like a shawl. It is generally three yards by forty eight inches, and the popular combination is muga (silk) mekhala and suti (cotton) chadar, with matching colors. The ensemble is used of course in addition to the blouse, the chadar being an extra cover for the upper part of the body. The mekhala is worn over a petticoat. This is for the unmarried woman.

After marriage the bride has an additional piece for the middle part—the riha, which is just a scarf with tasselled ends four yards long and twenty seven inches wide. This is wrapped around the waist to cover the midriff and guard against showing any part of it in case the blouse does not reach the waistline.

The dresses of each tribe have their own embellishments over the basic materials of the skirt and blouse. Some amount of Western influence on dress, due to direct contact with missionaries, is responsible for giving the final shape to the dresses of the tribal women of Assam. This is also true, for instance, of the Khasi people, whose traditional dress changed with the introduction of Christianity. Their dress was an inner piece of cloth fastened on the shoulders and draped tightly around the upper part of the body. The skirt was fastened to the waist with another piece of cloth serving as a belt. Over these was another piece in the traditional ensemble. It was made by tying two corners of the end of a cloth at the left shoulder, and passing the middle part of the end through the right side under the right arm and around the body. The other end of the cloth hung loosely down the body to the ankles. This traditional dress has been modified under Western influence. The dress which used to depend on the draping of a single piece of cloth was subjected to some tailoring. A chemise is now used next to the skin and the upper traditional piece is replaced by a blouse and tunic, based on the lines of the traditional upper garment. Western culture gives them the chemise, blouse, and also the frock. While working in the fields, Khasi women have a piece of cloth wound round the legs to protect them from leeches and thorns.

The hills, known as the Mikir, show some similarity with the Khasi region in respect to women's dress. The skirt is held to the waist with an ornamented girdle of strung silver coins. Another cloth is used to cover the upper body. A cloth is tied under the arms and drawn tightly over the breasts.

Very colorful and fascinating is the dress of women belonging to another tribe known as the Lakher. Their skirt is generally of cotton of deep blue color. The lower half of the skirt is embroidered in silk. Another shorter skirt is worn over the longer one so that only the upper part of the under-skirt is covered, and the lower half which is spectacularly embroidered is exposed. The upper skirt is also sometimes embroidered, and much care is taken to flaunt the embroidered designs in both skirts. The skirts used by ladies of royal descent are much more expensive, and decorated with shells and beads of various colors. Shining brass beads and the phosphorescent wings of a variety of green beetle are sometimes used to decorate these skirts. The skirts are held around the waist with belts which are of shining brass sections or bell-metal. The number of belts shows the rank of the wearer, and the number may be really large. The jacket for the upper part is worn so as to leave a small area of the midriff bare.

SHILLONG BEAUTY
Wrapped in a traditional chadar.

DRESSED FOR A TRIBAL DANCE

In the dancing costume, the chadar is carefully wrapped around the waist and tied to ensure free movement.

A NAGA COUPLE

A TYPICAL NAGA DRESS Modern trends are noticeable in the blouse, over which the sarong-type garment is wrapped in the usual manner.

NAGA FOLK DANCERS The horizontal stripes on the sarong-like garment of the Naga women are characteristic. In the background, a group of dancers.

YOUNG AND PRETTY

**The colorful costume and headdress
of a girl belonging to an Assam tribe.**

MANIPURI FABRICS

THE MODERN

The mekhala and chadar with some elegant touches to suit a role in a modern motion-picture.

NAGA EMBROIDERY

Beautiful embroidered cloths are made by Naga girls noted for their needle-work.

IN BRIDAL COSTUME

The bride's ensemble consists of mekhala, chadar, riha, and veil.

TEA GARDEN WORKER

Along with her colorful costume, this tea garden worker also loves ornaments. She wears earrings and beaded necklace of interesting design.

Bihar

GEOGRAPHICALLY, the state of Bihar forms part of a great area of the vast Indo-Gangetic plains. This area has a common language — Hindi. In Bihar, dress styles have followed more or less the lines set by people of the western parts of the plains area. The state's various tribes have their own distinctive styles of clothing each contributing its influence to a more general costume.

The state shares borders with Bengal in the east, Orissa in the south, and Nepal in the north. The border regions have mixed populations and therefore, their dress styles are influenced accordingly. The northern areas are moist and green, having medium to heavy rainfall resembling Bengal. The south and south-east are hilly, and covered by thick forests. In between, there are continuous stretches of comparatively arid and sun-scorched plains, with rainfall verging on scanty in some places. The river Ganges flows through the state as its main artery, and this, along with other deep rivers, provides water for a few patches of vegetation in this drought-stricken region. There is a comparative lack of color in the drier areas. This is compensated for with loud primary colors in which women's garments are dyed.

In contrast, most aborigines and tribal people in the state show a preference for white. White seems to dominate the dress of women. Their costumes are not so fascinating as those of Assam tribes, for they are quite simple, and even primitive in fabric and style, but are nevertheless remarkably artistic.

The regional characteristics of dress are absent from the standard sari-blouse ensemble of the educated and the urban, which follows a single pattern all over India. In the interior, however, the original styles of wearing the sari have been preserved.

This area has reached a happy medium by incorporating a blouse and the bodice. A sleeveless upper garment of this type is called a kurti. There are variations of this jacket, both sleeved and sleeveless, known by various local names. The best known among them is the choli.

In the Bihar style of draping the sari, the front pleats are gathered in a large bunch and tucked in at the waist. The emphasis on pleats is probably to make up for the original absence of any lower under garment corresponding to the petticoat. The petticoat is still absent among some groups. After being drawn across the shoulders, the free end of the sari is allowed to drape over the breast so as to display the showy fancy border (pallu) in full. In the Bengali style, the pallu is displayed half in the front, and half on the hip.

Married women wear a veil over the head as a sign of modesty. It is a separate piece, and great attention is paid to the veil in the entire Hindi speaking area. It is made of fine fabric and is elaborate with spangles and tinsel. The modern trend, however, is to discard the veil.

A most interesting group among the tribes is the Santhals because of their very artistic nature, their music, and their dances. Their modest huts, although having mud floors and walls, seem to breathe cleanliness. Their beauty is in their bareness.

To stick to traditions, the Santhal sari must be white, with a bright red border. The white saris with their red borders and graceful folds, are striking against the dark skins and the ochre background of the area.

The Santhal sari is generally six yards and worn to fall just below the knee. One end of it is wrapped round the loins, the surplus portion comes from the right side and passes over the left shoulder, leaving the right shoulder and arm free. The sari does not go over the head, and part of the right breast is exposed.

None of the tribes require their women to cover their head, either married or unmarried. There is no separate upper garment. The free end of the sari serves as a cover for the breast.

Contact with the so called civilized world, whose economic invasion is becoming unavoidable in rural India's struggle for existence, has made Santhal women imitate its ways and manners. I have met Santhal women wearing saris in all colors and designs, and also blouses and petticoats.

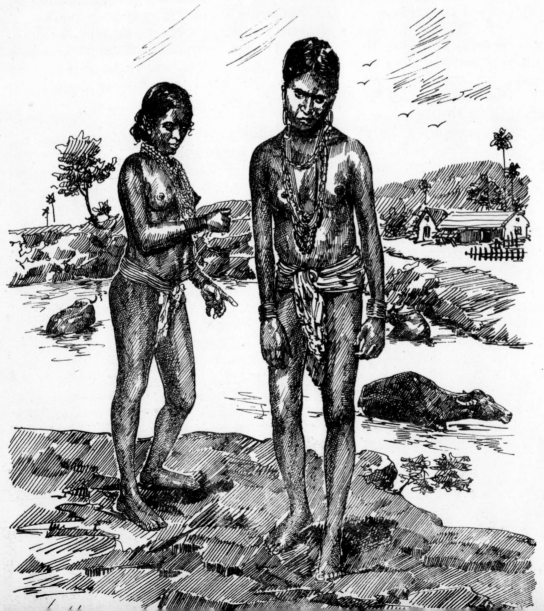

ABORIGINAL

Juang girls, in some parts of Bihar, are dressed almost as nature would have them be.

BIHAR VILLAGE WOMAN

The sari is worn in the Bihari style, with a kurti as an upper garment. The elaborate pleats and the decorative crosswise border are displayed on the front.

WORKING IN FIELDS

Village women at work in fields with their saris tightly wrapped and worn high above the ankles.

A NEW BRIDE

The sari is drawn over the head as a veil. The upper border of the free end of the sari thrown over the left shoulder in an additional sweep, shows a Muslim influence.

Uttar Pradesh

THE state we now enter can in many senses be called the heart of India, and it is perhaps not quite an unrelated fact that the hearts of all Indian women—at least the fashion conscious—belongs to this state, named Uttar Pradesh. For it is here that the sari of their dreams—the incomparable Banaras sari—is made. In India a bride's dream is to include a Banaras sari in her trousseau.

By now, the Banaras sari is no strange name to the women of the West, even those of the United States. It is amazing how American women touring India go into ecstasy looking at the better varieties of Banaras saris. Many of these fabulous saris are priced as high as a thousand dollars. I have noticed American women making it a point to include a Banaras sari in their Indian purchases.

There are hardly words to describe the beauty of this sari, a marvel of Indian craftsmanship, delicate and fine on one hand, gorgeous and rich on the other.

The state of Uttar Pradesh forms the core of what is known as Northern India. (Uttar—North, Pradesh — Province). Historically, Northern India has been the melting pot where cultures of different lands and peoples met. From this a new culture was born, a culture that later came to dominate in India. The important periods of Hindu India were based in this area, and the contact with the Muslims also had its nucleus in Northern India. It is mainly here that the assimilation of different cultures happened to form the present day dress of India.

The capital, Lucknow, is an old city and in the latter days of Muslim India, when the glory of Delhi and Agra was on the wane, it became the country's cultural center. It is still so to a major section, known as the Hindi area, the largest single cultural unit in the country. To the Indian costume, the contribution of Lucknow is great, the most important contribution being the Lucknow chicon. The chicon is a fine white embroidery noted for its simplicity. It is worn by ladies of refinement and good taste.

Uttar Pradesh is important in the history of Indian Costumes because it is here that Muslim and Hindu cultures had the happiest blend, and the dress of the Indian women today has a basic element borrowed from the Muslims. It is the tailored garment. Of the characteristic Indian ensemble, the sari, petticoat and blouse, only the sari is Hindu. The blouse and petticoat of the ensemble were foreign to India. Long contact with the Muslims made Indians realise the utility of sewn garments, and so things like ghagra and choli were accepted by the Hindu women. The modern petticoat and blouse have descended from ghagra and choli respectively.

Uttar Pradesh, along with the adjacent states, Bihar, Rajasthan and Madhya Pradesh, makes up an area marked greatly by similarity of habits and manners, due to a common speech—Hindi. The dress ensembles of this area come under two styles, one being the ghagra, choli and orhna; and the other the sari and blouse.

The ghagra has its own area where it predominates or even has a monopoly as does the sari and blouse in others. Uttar Pradesh which is mainly a sari area, has overlappings of the ghagra too.

The ghagra, a full skirt reaching to the ankles from the waist, and copiously pleated, is discussed in the chapter relevant to it. It is worn with a breast piece, and an orhna—which is a short piece of decorative cloth used to cover the bare portions of the anatomy left uncovered by the skirt and the upper piece.

In the sari and blouse ensemble, the state has much in common with the neighboring state, Bihar. The ways of wearing the sari and blouse among educated Hindus in both states are identical. One end of the sari is wrapped around the waist and tucked. The front pleats are done with great care, and are gathered and neatly tied to form a knot. The free end of the sari comes from the left hip up the back and over the head. It then falls on the bosom from over the right shoulder. In all the Hindi areas the showy crosswise border is displayed wholly on the front.

There are two kinds of saris in vogue in the area: one is of the standard length—about five and a half yards. The other is of a shorter

LEFT OR RIGHT ?

Usually, the left arm is free in the Uttar Pradesh sari style. The modern tendency is to reverse the wrap as seen in the sari of the bride.

length, and it takes great skill to drape the shorter sari properly. The orhna, an addi- tional piece, is used to make up for the short length of this kind of sari.

STYLES OF THE STATE
Uttar Pradesh lady dressed in an expensive silk sari in a style popular in the state.

HIGH AND LOW A washerwoman, a peasant, and a lady of higher caste, dressed according to status.

VINTAGE COSTUME
From an old photograph showing design and style, with ornaments in vogue over 80 years ago.

WORK AHEAD
On the way to work in the field. The sari shows a distinctive Uttar Pradesh style in the front pleats and the veil. The left hand is free.

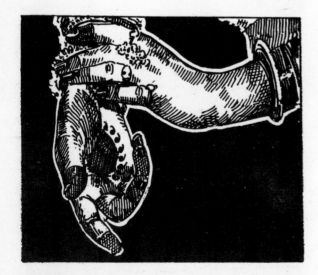

BRIDAL PAINT

The designs on the bride's hands and feet are made with a dye called mehendi, believed to have a magic effect on the marriage.

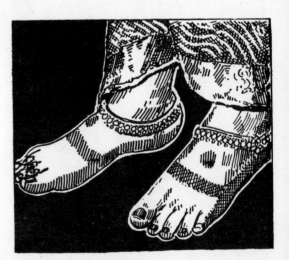

ADORNED FEET

The anklets and other foot ornaments add grace and romance to the bride's beauty.

NEW BRIDE

The sari is Banaras, a wedding gift. The nose ornament is customary, but the bride does not continue to wear it after the wedding ceremony.

Rajasthan

COLOR is as important to the people of Rajasthan as the very precious water, which is scarce in this very dry state. Except for the few green areas, where high mountains and deep forests abound, the state is very barren, with vast stretches of sand known as the Indian desert. Drab tones dominate most of the landscape. The monotony is relieved, however, by the bright and vivid colors of the regional costumes.

Much of the charm of old Rajasthani paintings which have survived for centuries, derives from the exquisite portrayals of Rajput women in their colorful attire.

Rajasthan, meaning land of kings and princes, is a name that conjures up a past crowded with heroic exploits of valiant warriors. Closely linked with these are stories of heroic women whose achievements matched their men's. The chivalry of these Rajasthani kings has been celebrated by native poets as well as western historians. Their women could be strong in times of need, but they were nevertheless romantic. Their traditional costumes still retain the features which were in keeping with those traits of Rajasthani women.

The ghagra, a pleated full skirt, described earlier, can be said to be the universal costume of the Rajasthani woman, although she is not totally averse to wearing the sari. In fact there is today a liking for the sari, particularly those women who have had the opportunity to travel to other parts of the country. In West Bengal, where there is a considerable Rajasthani population, particularly in the capital city of Calcutta, it is usual to see Rajasthani women dressed almost exclusively in saris, except on ceremonial occasions. Their saris, however, bear distinctive evidence of their color preferences, including embroidered or woven floral designs, and some very exclusive prints are worn.

The ghagra, with the tight bodice worn with it, is a practical dress, eminently suited to the woman who could also wield the sword. The ghagra gave her the poise and freedom of movement that she needed. It is a pleasure today to see a village woman of Rajasthan dressed in ghagra, choli and orhna, with a number of pails full of water balanced on her head, in tiers. They can walk gracefully for miles, without ever touching the pails.

The short-sleeved bodice of the Rajasthani woman is generally open at the back, and fastened with tie strings. The coveredback type choli, which is more recent, is also very popular.

The ghagra is elaborately pleated and is made by sewing up a number of triangular pieces—usually sixty-four or more, each being called a kali, or petal of a flower. It sometimes takes twenty-five yards of cloth to make a single ghagra.

The most important piece in the Rajasthani woman's ensemble is the scarf, or orhna. It is used as a veil as well as a decorative piece, to give continuity to the ghagra and bodice because here the ghagra is worn below the navel. The bodice is short enough to leave part of the midriff bare, so the orhna serves to bridge the gap.

The women of Rajasthan greatly enjoy festivals. There are a number of these celebrated throughout the year, and in no other part of India are the women so particular about joining in all of the events. They assemble in large groups, on the occasion of each festival, and sing traditional songs which are inseparable parts of the festivity. What is most striking in all this, is that they take the greatest care to dress according to each festival. Traditional costumes are prescribed for each, and great care is taken to follow the rules established through tradition.

Some of the songs they sing are composed in praise of the orhna because it occupies a great place in the heart of Rajasthani women. The sweetest songs are those that tell of the scarf. It is called the chunari. The Rajasthani girl believes that a lot depends on the wedding chunari for the success of her marriage. Brides strive to choose the right color and designed chunari in order to win the heart of a husband.

One of the most important festivals is the invocation of the rains during the monsoon season. Women of all ages take part in it. For days hopeful eyes look up only to see a copper colored sky. (In 1970, a district in Rajasthan named Jaishalmere had its first drop of rain in seven years). It is during these sun-scorched days that the women sing and pray to the rain god. For this festival, the color of the ghagra is bright orange, and the number of pleats is sixty-four. The accompanying orhna is rippled with wavy designs.

Women of the upper classes wear a narrow piece of cloth over the front of the ghagra. Its color and design differ from those of the ghagra. This is a traditional custom, indicating that the wearer's husband is living.

Conservative married women of high families wear an additional white covering when going out. The scarf or orhna is drawn over the face to show respect to certain elders. This is a characteristic which the Rajasthani woman shares with most other Indian women. Here however, her sense of modesty is gauged by the length of the scarf.

BALANCING TRICK

There is no trick, however. It is her posture which keeps the pails balanced on the head of the Rajasthani girl.

BRIDE OF RAJASTHAN The sleeved short choli and orhna are richly decorated for the bride.

HOW DO I LOOK?
The coy bride has only herself to ask.

WORTH HER WEIGHT
The love of ornaments sometimes assumes absurd proportions in parts of India, as seen in the weight of metal decorations worn by this Rajasthani woman.

MIRRORED DESIGN
A Rajasthani fabric with small pieces of mirrors, diamond shaped or round, worked into the embroidered design.

EMBROIDERED NAGRAS
Nagras are Indian shoes worn by both men and women.

ON WAY TO FIELD
The ornaments worn by the Rajasthani village woman are indicative of her married status.

WAITING FOR HER MAN The jacket this Rajasthani woman wears is different from the short choli usually seen.

**A RAJASTHANI
BEAUTY**

Gujarat

THE domain of the ghagra, a pleated full skirt, stretches beyond Rajasthan in the west and southwest to Gujarat along the coast of the Arabian Sea. Gujarat has a mixture of costumes, with the ghagra and sari both popular.

The state of Gujarat derives its name from the predominating linguistic group speaking Gujarati. Geographically it also includes a large area named Sourashtra, which culturally and historically has a distinct identity. In Sourashtra, particularly among the peasant and working classes, the ghagra is almost the exclusive dress.

Elsewhere, the sari keeps growing in popularity. But it has not totally replaced the ghagra, which still exists as an undergarment over which the sari is worn.

The sari, of course, is usually worn over a petticoat. The difference here is that the petticoat of the Gujarati woman is tailored with greater care. Normally the petticoat used as an undergarment has only a few pleats and a minimum of embroidery and decorative borders. But the Gujarati ladies have their petticoats gaily embellished as the ghagra was when it was used as the main garment.

In the Gujarati style of wearing the sari, the front pleats are important, as elsewhere in northern India, and the same is true of the manner of showing the elegant crosswise border. It is displayed wholly on the front (unlike the Bengali way of wearing the border, half in front and half on the hip, or the southern way where the decorative border is displayed wholly on the hip). The front pleats are either tucked into the petticoat or tied in a knot.

The Gujarati sari is five yards in length and more than half of this goes for the wrap and the pleats. Of the remaining portion, a part is used to form a crescent over the left hip. The rest is then used to cover the back and head, and fall over the right shoulder. The left corner of the portion thus brought to the front over the shoulder, is drawn to the left waist, to display the beautiful crosswise border. The right hand of the wearer remains covered and the left hand is exposed.

The choli worn with the sari is open-backed, and fastened with two strings drawn across the back. The open-backed choli eventually is replaced by the covered back type fastening in front, as the wearer grows older.

The saris of the Gujarati ladies are richly bordered, but woven borders are not for them. They prefer borders that are either printed or sewn on along the entire length.

In this part of India, brides wear red saris with multicolored borders on white backgrounds. Gujarati women like variety in their collections of saris. They use silks with many colors on white backgrounds in the crosswise borders. Another favorite is red silk with silver borders.

The ghagras used by the peasant women are generally without pleats, and made from rectangular pieces of cloth. The color preferred by these women is reddish brown. There may be pleats, but they are optional. The ghagra is worn with a back-fastening bodice, with sleeves sometimes reaching beyond the elbow. The abdomen is liberally exposed and the scarf or orhna does not cover the bare midriff, but rests on the head and back, partially covering the bosom. Sometimes it is placed on the head like a hood, and tucked into the bodice.

The ghagra of Gujarat differs from that of Rajasthan in some places, but the elaborately pleated Rajasthan type is also seen here and there. Another variety of ghagra is fashioned out of five different pieces and of five different colors. This garment is most colorful.

The scarf worn with the ghagra is not of a uniform length. In some areas the scarf is rather long, and resembles a sari. These long scarves are also worn somewhat in the manner of the sari.

The speciality of the Gujarati orhna is in its multicolored design. Sometimes as many as a hundred different shades are used.

THE PATOLA

Fabrics of Gujarat are famous for the beautiful designs woven into the texture by a process indigenous to the region.

IN BRIDAL COSTUME

TRIBAL TYPES

No revolution in headdress this, but bundles of sticks for fuel balanced on the head. Women of this tribe of Gujarat are hard-working. They mind their children while working outdoors.

THE THREE GRACES

Charming in their pristine freshness and simple costumes, the three girls represent another of the many tribes of Gujarat.

Maharashtra

THE geo-political areas covered so far have one common feature in the wearing of the sari—about one half of the sari is wrapped, from one end, around the waist to form a skirt.

In the west, however, south of Gujarat, one finds a sari style radically different from those collectively considered by Europeans and other foreigners to be the norm. The difference, which I shall describe, is such that it divides the entire sari area of India into two regions, or zones: north and south.

The southern zone includes a very important state, Maharashtra, whose capital is Bombay, the second largest of India's four metropolitan cities, and the most westernized of them all. Here, the sari is made from material almost twice the length common in the northern zone, being up to eleven yards long, as against six yards elsewhere, and also somewhat wider, with a narrow border. This unusual length is needed to swaddle the right thigh, giving the resultant sari a trouserlike utility.

The first wrap is taken from a portion of the middle of the long length of cloth. After the latter is fastened at the waist, there are two free ends, one to the right and the other to the left. The right length is pleated along part of the top border, and tucked in at the waist, in front. The remainder is passed to the rear between the legs, drawn up tight, pleated, and tucked in also at the waist, but in the middle of the back. The second wrap—from the left length—drapes the torso in a similar fashion to the sari worn in the north.

The pleats at the back are called the kachha. It is interesting to note that the kachha is a feature of men's national dress—the dhoti. There is an old joke in Bengal that women cannot make a kachha even with a six-yard cloth, implying that women are less resourceful and intelligent than men. Now that travel is becoming easier, that joke will fade out as Bengali men find that Maharashtrian women use the kachhas in draping their saris.

This style gives its wearers freedom of movement, although it has one drawback in that it exposes the back of the leg from the calf to the knee. There are style varieties, particularly for manual laborers, in which the end of the cloth, after swathing the thigh, does not fall much below the knee so that the flowing end can be drawn up from behind to drape over the head. According to existing portraits of Maharashtrian female warriors, the same style was favored by the many heroines who fought alongside their men in battle through several periods of Indian history.

The bodice is similar to those seen elsewhere in India, although here it leaves much of the upper abdomen bare. The main part of the sari, however, provides complete concealment.

Maharashtrian women love colored and patterned borders in their saris. As a result, there are a great many types of saris named after these patterns, which are seen in numerous color combinations. As mentioned above, relatively narrow borders are preferred, even by married women.

GOING VISITING

Maharashtrian family off for a
visit to her parents.

FISHERWOMAN

She loves ornaments and colorful saris, and dresses with care before going out to sell fish.

ON THE WAY TO TEMPLE

Her sari shows the rear pleats characteristic of Maharashtra.

A NEW WORLD

The bride in her wedding costume enters her husband's home, the house of her father-in-law.

TRADITIONAL
BRIDAL COSTUME
**Small figure shows the "kachha" or
pleats tucked in rear.**

Punjab

IN order to see women in form-fitting clothing, one must go to the north-west of India, in the states of Himachal Pradesh, Kashmir, and Punjab. There, women generally wear a three-piece ensemble, in which upper and lower garments are tailored to the shape of the body.

Punjab is known to westerners as the home of the Sikhs, whose stately men tie up their beards in a net, and top their heads in an imposing turban. Their women dress in salwar, kameez, and dupatta, of which the kameez is the blouse-like upper garment, sometimes form-fitting to the point of being skin tight. Both men and women wear a salwar, or trousers, but the ladies' version is longer, generally made of finer and richer material, and varies from loose to form-fitting according to fashion or individual taste. The dupatta, also known as orhna, is a flowing scarf of fine cloth, usually about four and a half feet long, resting on the shoulders, with the middle portion draped low to cover the bosom.

The kameez has long sleeves tapered to the wrists. Sometimes the skirt is flared below the waist. The salwar is generally white, although for evening wear it is occasionally black or some other solid color. In the case of bridal dress, the salwar is extra long, covering the feet almost to the toes.

It is an interesting fact that this garb is the dress of both Hindu and Muslim women in the north-western states, whereas in the rest of the country it is the customary attire of Muslim ladies only. The kameez is a fairly recent addition to this native costume (perhaps derived from the chemise in form and name). Formerly, also, the skirt-like ghagra that is the main garment of Rajasthani women was associated with Punjab. Except for bridal wear, where the ghagra is worn over the salwar, it has long been out of fashion here, although it was retained for some time by conservative families. The dupatta is reminiscent of the veil worn with the ghagra in Rajasthan.

Indians speak of their country as being characterized by possessing unity in diversity. This is evident in regional dress customs that influence styles in neighboring areas, and provide a reservoir for fashion throughout the country. The salwar-kameez ensemble may appear strange or even foreign to women who are accustomed to wearing a sari, or a ghagra, yet it is now natural to see an educated Bengali woman wearing the latest fashion in kameez and salwar, or a Punjabi lady elegantly dressed for a social occasion in choli and sari.

Although the sari has been an important unifying factor in national dress, the women of the north-west, as elsewhere, have resisted its influence. The salwar-kameez ensemble has tremendous appeal, in fact it appears to be the teen-agers' choice, and were it not for its requirement of a good figure, it might have become the alternative national dress for Indian women.

BRIDE WITH HER NEW SISTER-IN-LAW

In Punjab the bride's salwar is long and almost covers the feet.

WEDDING SONGS
Women who attend wedding ceremonies enjoy singing traditional songs.

GAY HANDS AND FEET
As elsewhere in India, Punjabi women have charming designs painted on their hands and feet.

PUNJABI BRIDE IN SALWAR AND KAMEEZ

The nose-ring held by a chain, and the bracelets are part of the bridal costume.

PHULKARI
An embroidered fabric of Punjab
noted for its artistic designs.

A PUNJABI BELLE

Kashmir

KASHMIR, the northernmost state of India, is called the Switzerland of Asia by well travelled Indians. The valley, its lakes and grasslands surrounded by gorgeous snow-capped mountains, make Kashmir one of the loveliest spots on the globe. Beauty is everywhere in the landscape, in the perfect features of its people, and in the exquisite handwork done by its craftsmen. It is in Shrinagar, the capital city, that the famous gardens of Shalimar (the abode of love) are found. Poets, musicians, and painters are inspired by the natural beauty of Kashmir.

Originally a Hindu kingdom, Kashmir came to be predominantly Muslim in recent times. Through successive periods of history—Hindu, Buddhist and Muslim—its culture, mode of dress, handicrafts, and ways of life were naturally influenced. The blend of various elements is also noticed in the costumes. Kashmir is one place in India where Hindu and Muslim dress the same. Elsewhere in the country conservative Muslims strictly adhere to tradition. In Kashmir, the Muslim women are free and there is no purdah system.

The Muslim influence is very evident in Kashmir costumes. The salwar, somewhat like that seen in Punjab, is the main lower garment of both the male and female. It may be fitted or gathered, similar to those popular in Afghanistan. The Kashmiri salwar sometimes has beautifully embroidered borders at the ankles. The upper garment, called a pheran, is a full gown which hangs in loose folds and has sleeves. This covers an under garment.

A sleeveless jacket of embroidered velvet of a dark shade is occasionally used over the gown. A scarf similar to the orhna of Rajasthan and Punjab, but different in quality and design, completes the clothing outfit.

A skull cap with fine embroidery is the typical head-dress. Usually the Kashmiri lady tucks her scarf into the cap, but not as a veil of modesty. However, it is customary for a bride to wear a veil at her wedding, and her cap is elaborately embroidered and adorned with lace. Dresses for both Muslim and Hindu brides are the same, but the head-dress shows a slight difference. The Hindu bridal cap, called a taranga, is somewhat more decorative than the kasaba or Muslim cap.

In days gone by the skill and incomparable craftsmanship required to make the best shawls for great Mughals was incredible. These brought fabulous prices, and now that these princely pieces have ceased to be woven, they are rare collectors' items.

The finest Kashmiri shawls are made from the wool of a species of hill goat. Only the soft wool from the belly is used. Sheep's wool is also used for less expensive varieties. This wool may be used pure or mixed with silk.

The embroidered designs are based on the natural characteristics of the area. The most widely used pattern is the leaf of the chenar tree which grows abundantly in Kashmir. Apple blossoms, almond nuts, and various bird motifs are also popular. Jamaivar, a variety of brocaded wool is also made in Kashmir. This cloth may be of pure wool or mixed with cotton. Floral designs in silk, or silk and wool, are worked in the fabric.

Although the sari is not widely used here, Kashmir is famous for its beautifully printed silks popular in all parts of India.

BEAUTY OF THE LAKE

A lady of Kashmir in her salwar, pheran and cap, glides across one of the beautiful lakes in a small primitive craft.

TIME FOR MEDITATION

SUNSHINE ON DAL LAKE

THE MAGIC OF THE NEEDLE
Kashmiri shawls are noted for exquisite embroidery work hand done by the craftsmen.

SHAWL EMBROIDERY
Such designs are embroidered on shawls extempore without drawings or patterns.

EARRINGS GALORE

The Kashmiri girl loves bunches of
elaborate earrings.

Himachal Pradesh

WHEN designers of London fashioned a costume to suit both sexes I thought that this was not new to India. During one of my journeys within the country, I met a couple and was amazed to see that husband and wife were dressed almost alike. They came from a district in the hilly state of Himachal Pradesh. This north-western state, bordering Kashmir, is in the Himalayan mountain range. These people belonged to a tribe known as Gaddi, from the section called Chambal, and are one of the many colorful ethnic groups populating Himachal Pradesh.

An interesting feature of the Gaddi tribes is the "unisex" dress which is called chola. Its length reaches the ankles and it is so loose that it is said that a shepherd can carry four lambs in the baggy upper portion when a woolen string is tied around the waist.

The chola of the women is the same. It is generally woolen, for comfort in the cold climate, but cotton gowns have also become popular. The wool for the chola is locally produced and is rather coarse. Since the gown reaches from neck to ankle no under garment is necessary. However, tight trousers can be seen peeping from below the bottom, in recent days.

Because of the freezing winters the Gaddis wear an oval shaped cap on their heads. The cap may be richly decorated with beads, feathers or silver ornaments.

Himachal Pradesh matches Kashmir in natural beauty and has a bracing cold climate. Some of the picturesque resorts are Delhousie, Kangra Valley, Kulu Valley and Simla. Simla is known as the summer capital of India. A famous school of Indian painting is found in Kangra.

The long pheran and salwar used in Kashmir are also popular in Himachal Pradesh, but tribal groups have their own distinctive costumes. These people live a simple life in pastoral settings and fairs and folk dances are of great importance in their traditional festivals. For these occasions their dancing costumes are fascinating in both color and design.

A BEVY OF HIMACHAL BEAUTIES

THE CHAMBA COSTUME

The chola, an ample gown reaching the ankles, is the common dress of Chamba in Himachal Pradesh.

A TYPICAL HIMACHAL PRADESH BELLE

The ornaments are as interesting as the costume.

South India

THE "Deep South" of India consists geographically of the four main states between Maharashtra (which is still considered to be a southern state) and the tip of the subcontinent. This part of the country is referred to by northerns as South India. The languages of this region may be considered a family or group quite different from those of the North. The culture of the area, at least insofar as it is expressed in dress, manners, and customs, is also different, in spite of the importance of the Hindu religion as a cultural link between the North and South.

The four states are Andhra Pradesh, Tamilnadu, Mysore, and Kerala, and the languages that provide the principal basis for their creation are, respectively, Telugu, Tamil, Kannada, and Malayalam.

The long sari in women's dress is the one link between Maharashtra and the other southern states. Whereas in the North, the sari is nowhere more than six yards, in these five states the minimum length is seven yards and the maximum is about ten. Except in Kerala, women of the southern states have adopted, with variations, of course, the practice of drawing pleats to the rear, through the legs, as in Maharashtra. This fashion is seen here, however, on special occasions only.

In Andhra Pradesh, the sari is fashioned from about eight yards of material, and usually it is worn with pleats in front. For members taking part in wedding rituals the pleats are drawn behind, and tucked in at the waist. There are several ways of draping the upper body. One is to draw the free end of the material up from the right thigh, across the bosom, and over the left shoulder, where it falls loose except for one corner, which is tucked in at the right side of the waist, thus draping a part of the back. Another way is to reverse the direction from that just described. In any case, the sari here does not include a portion drawn over the head, like a hood.

In Tamilnadu, there are several variants of the sari, for which different lengths of material are required—from seven to ten yards. The pleats that are drawn to the rear for tucking at the waist, are covered by an additional wrap so as to conceal them except for a few inches at the ankle. As in Andhra, there are two main ways of draping the torso—from right to left, and vice versa. A popular style here is to drape the material from the left, across the bosom, and over the right shoulder. The free end is passed around the neck to return to the front over the left shoulder. After that, it crosses the bosom again, to go under the right arm. In Tamilnadu the choli type of bodice, and its modern version, the blouse, are comparatively recent additions to native dress.

In Mysore, saris are fashioned from material nine to ten yards long. While generally some of this great length is used up in pleats at the rear, the style is not practiced universally. However, it is prescribed for married women taking part in religious ceremonies, and there are a few other occasions when it is customarily followed.

The Malayalam area has its own traditional dress style, which is not related to those of the other three states of the Deep South. Within this style there are varying modes, depending on the caste of the wearer. In all cases, the entire length of material is wrapped around the waist with numerous pleats, like a skirt, and none is left for draping the torso. The skirt is topped with a blouse, and a short scarf-like piece is thrown over the shoulders. In modern times, most ladies have adopted the all-India sari and choli style.

South Indian saris are noted for their striking colors, whether matched or contrasting, and they have charming motifs for their crosswise borders. They are popular all over India, although they do not have the elegance, or class, of the Banaras sari. Their popularity may be noted, for example, in West Bengal during September at the approach of India's most popular festival, Dusserah, which in Bengal is celebrated as Durga Puja. Here the fabric shops resound with a babel of place-names for saris, and almost nine out of ten are the styles of the Deep South—Conjeevaram, Coimbatore, Bangalore, Aurangabad, Venkat-giri, and many others.

SOUTH INDIAN COSTUME AND JEWELRY

MIDDLE-AGED WOMAN
The style of her sari is typically south Indian.

**DRESSED FOR
HER WEDDING**

Muslim Costumes

BRIDAL COSTUME

The head-covering used as a veil and a symbol of modesty is believed to have been originated by the Muslims.

MUSLIM ARISTOCRACY

Bride of a wealthy family of Lucknow dressed according to the tradition of her family.

CASUAL AND INDOOR WEAR

Mughal Costumes

PALACE FASHIONS

Mumtaz Mahal, consort of Emperor Shahjahan, over whose grave stands the Taj Mahal. Right: Emperor Shahjahan, the most stylish of the Mughals, and a leader of fashion.

Emperor Jahangir, father of Shahjahan. Right: Jodha Bai, mother of Jahangir.

Buddhist Period

BUDDHA IMAGE

FROM AJANTA WALL PAINTINGS

A COSTUME REMADE EXACTLY FROM AN AJANTA PAINTING

Costumes for Dancers

MANIPURI

A dance of Manipur, the easternmost territory of India. The stiff skirts with rich embroidery are unique features of this dance.

KATHAK

A dance of Northern India for which salwars are essential.

KATHAKALI

A dance of Kerala performed with masks and colorful dresses.

ORISI DANCER
In typical pose.

BHARAT NATYAM
Expressive hands.

BHARAT NATYAM
A south Indian dancer in pleated sari.

Traditional Ornaments

1. Necklace
2. Earring
3. Nosering
4. Ring

5. Necklace
6. Bangle
7. Bracelet
8. Toering

The Indian woman loves her ornaments. So much so that she has a piece for virtually every limb. The ornaments have material as well as symbolic value in her life. She measures her husband's (or any one's) love for her in the value of the ornaments he buys her. On the other hand her love for her husband and children stands the severest test when she parts with her ornaments for them in times of emergency. Gold and silver are the metals she likes. The preference for jewelry is not universal.

Top: Tussar Silk
Bottom: Printed Silk

Banaras Silk

THE most striking modern fashions are based on the Punjabi salwar and kameez, which are popular with teenagers. The kameez and orhna (Right) are of printed handlooms, the kameez tapering to the knees instead of being flared. Below: another variation of the kameez fitting the figure like a sheath.

Modern Day

Salwar, kameez, and sleeveless
embroidered jacket.

The printed voile is the most popular
summer wear of today.

Salwar and kameez with a long orhna
used as a wrapper.

Typical Male Costumes

Left to Right:

Short pyjama, kurta and English coat; churidar, achkan and cap.

Left to Right :

Dhoti, kurta and chadar; gathered pyjama, shirt, English coat and pugree; churidar, achkan and pugree.

GLOSSARY

Achkan—Long high-necked, closed-breast coat (male) slightly flared at knee, with a long row of front buttons.

Anchla—Decorative crosswise border, of cloth used as main lower garment of women.

Blouse—Main upper garment of Indian women.

Bodice—Close-fitting upper garment down to waist.

Brahma—Monotheistic sect founded in early XIXth Century by members of the Hindu community who did not believe in idolatry.

Brassier—Women's breast support.

Burkha—Bell-shaped full veil with holes for eyes used by conservative Muslim ladies.

Chadar—Rectangular piece of cloth used as wrapper.

Chenar Tree—Tree, with leaves resembling those of ivy, abundant in Kashmir.

Chicon—White embroidery done on white muslin. Also may be colored.

Chola—Long ample gown reaching to ankles worn by men as well as women in parts of north-western India.

Choli—Originally indigenous breast-garment. Now used as blouse over brassier.

Chunari—See Dupatta.

Churidar—Tight trousers.

Dhoti—Length of cotton worn by male Hindus as main lower garment.

Dupatta—Scarf draped over main upper garment.

Extinguisher—Veil to cover face by drawing portion of cloth resting on head.

Ghagra—Pleated full skirt reaching ankles.

Hindu—Indian professing Hinduism, the religion of the majority, marked by idol worship and belief in many gods.

Jamaivar—Embroidered woolen or mixed yarn wrapper, made in Kashmir.

Kaccha—Pleated end of sari drawn between legs from front to rear, and tucked in at the waist.

Kachuli—Indigenous bodice, used as breast-garment.

Kameez—Long tunic flared at knees and with tapering sleeves, worn as main upper garment in Punjab and adjacent areas.

Kasaba—Muslim bride's cap of Kashmir.

Kurta—Light tunic, generally of fine muslin flared at the bottom end, with loose or tapering sleeves, worn by males in north India.

Kurti—Indigenous bodice of Bihar.

Mekhala—Straight skirt reaching to ankles worn by women of Assam.

Meter—39.37 inches.

Muga—A variety of silk from the cocoon of moths of the same name. Produced in Assam.

Mughal—A Muslim dynasty of India founded in 1526 and existing till 1857.

Muslim—Follower of Islam; Mohammmedan.

Orhna—See Dupatta.

Pallu—See Anchla

Petticoat—Inner skirt worn as undergarment for sari.

Pugree—Headdress of Indian male; turban.

Riha—Length of cloth for waist required by married Assamese women.

Salwar—Tapering trousers of women of Punjab, Kashmir and adjacent areas.

Sari—Length of cotton or silk, draped around body, used as the main lower garment by most Indian women.

Sarong—Javanese women's dress; a length of cloth wrapped around breast under the armpits, and reaching halfway to ankle.

Sikh—Member of Indian community founded as monotheistic sect *c.* 1500 in Punjab.

Sola—White pith of tropical swamp plant.

Suti—Cotton yarn.

Taranga—Hindu bride's cap of Kashmir.

Unisex—Dress suitable for both sexes.